JIGSAW

A compilation of poems
written by people affected by Parkinson's Disease

Jan Sargeant

Copyright: The Contributors, 2020
All rights reserved

ISBN: 978-1-71663-399-7

Published by lulu.com

Cover Image by Vicky Grainger
Typeset by John Schwartz

All proceeds from the sale of this book will be donated to Parkinsons's UK.

Should the reader wish to add a donation they should send a cheque to:

Parkinson's UK
215 Vauxhall Bridge Road
LONDON
SW1V 1EJ
Quoting the following number: 910286

OR

By telephoning 0800 1386593
Quoting the following number: 910286

This book of poems is dedicated to all those affected by Parkinson's Disease, be they people with the condition, their carers or family members.

ACKNOWLEDGEMENTS

The work that has gone into producing this book cannot be attributed to one person. It is the culmination of the efforts, the talents and the artistic flair of many individuals. I applaud them all for their faith in this project, for their open and honest approach to the debilitating disease that is Parkinson's and for their faith in a project which, at first glance seemed impossible. Your courage in opening up your innermost emotions is both amazing and humbling. Thank you for your courage and the support you give each other.

I also wish to thank the following persons for the contribution they have made. Gary Shaughnessy who, on behalf of Parkinson's UK has supported our efforts to raise awareness of Parkinson's Disease which affects us all, whether we have Parkinson's or are a carer to someone with this disease. To Al Ferber, for the generous gift of his poem "Dark River" and his support of our writing. Vicky Grainger for graciously gifting her design of the book cover and thereby establishing the book's title of "Jigsaw". A big thank you to our photographers and artists who have provided the illustrations in the book (you know who you are!) To John Schwartz for technical support and advice. We couldn't have done it without you. And finally to my fellow editor, Jan Sargeant for her editing skills, constructive criticism, optimism and her belief that we would reach our goal.

I thank you all.

JENNIFER YATES, August 2020

CONTENTS

Preface | *Gary Shaughnessy*   xi

Your Voice | *Jennifer Yates*   1
To a Carer | *Jan Sargeant*   2
Four Seasons | *Jan Sargeant*   3
Dark River | *Al Ferber*   5
Trees | *Debbie Williams*   7
Cuckoo | *Joy Lloyd*   8
Moon Gazing | *Jennifer Yates*   10
Then There Were Three | *Jennifer Yates*   11
Fabric –ation | *Jan Sargeant*   12
The Bed I Longed to Climb into | *Carol Bowden*   13
Bubbles Before Breakfast | *Debbie Williams*   14
It's a Bugger When … | *Jan Sargeant*   15
The Selfless Act of Giving | *Jennifer Yates*   16
I Really Didn't Want You | *Carol Bowden*   18
Silly O'Clock | *Karen Browne*   20
Cheese on Toast | *Colin Pidgely*   21
The Life Of an Administrator | *Carol Bowden*   22
Kids Today | *Barry Wiggins*   23

British Justice | *Jan Sargeant*		24
Mr Parkinson's | *Barry Wiggins*		25
Ghost Ship | *Barry Wiggins*		26
PC | *Jan Sargeant*		27
Castle Urquhart | *Jennifer Yates*		28
Handbags on Noses | *Barry Wiggins*		30
When Robots Start to Die | *Barry Wiggins*		31
Love Letters | *Jennifer Yates*		32
Words | *Jan Sargeant*		33
My Daily Battle | *Andy Clegg*		34
Wearing the Red Rose | *Barry Wiggins*		35
Hold My Hand | *Carol Bowden*		37
Tell the Truth | *Jan Sargeant*		38
Parkinson's | *Joy Lloyd*		39
Seed Head | *Jan Sargeant*		41
After the Rain | *Joy Lloyd*		42
Chameleon | *Jan Sargeant*		43
Autumn | *Debbie Williams*		44
On African Plains | *Andy Clegg*		45
Mr PD | *Hazel Morgan*		46
Palindrome | *Barry Wiggins*		48
Practising the Form | *Jennifer Yates*		50
Pillows and Pills | *Colin Pidgley*		49
The Moment | *Barry Wiggins*		52
The Iron Horse | *Barry Wiggins*		53

Paint me a Poem | *Jennifer Yates*	54
Growing Older with Parkinson's | *Jan Sargeant*	55
Field of Dreams | *Barry Wiggins*	56
No Going Back | *Jan Sargeant*	57
Invisible Light | *Jennifer Yates*	59
No Party | *Jennifer Yates*	60
Rhythm of Life | *Jan Sargeant*	62
A Step Too Far | *Jennifer Yates*	64
Dopamine Blues | *Jennifer Yates*	65
Baggage Collectors | *Jan Sargeant*	66
Dysnomia | *Jennifer Yates*	67
Lost Sense | *Sally Church*	68
The Painter | *Colin Pidgley*	69
Triad of Dragons | *Jennifer Yates*	70
My Dear | *Joy Lloyd*	73
The Artist | *Jennifer Yates*	74
A Point at the End | *Jan Sargeant*	75
Jigsaw Puzzle | *Jan Sargeant & Jennifer Yates*	76
Web Spinners | *Jan Sargeant & Jennifer Yates*	79
The Painting: Possession or Possessed | *Jan Sargeant & Jennifer Yates*	80
Cliffhanger | *Jan Sargeant & Jennifer Yates*	82
Pink Hares | *Jan Sargeant & Jennifer Yates*	84

PREFACE

When I was diagnosed with Parkinson's, my immediate reaction was wholly negative. Now, six years later, I still wish I hadn't got the condition, but I've come to admire and try to learn from the many brilliant and resilient people in the Parkinson's community that I wouldn't have met otherwise.

By combining their poems and their art work, the contributors all find a way to bring life to what it means to live with Parkinson's – something that's so difficult to explain to those who don't experience it. That life can be sad, frustrating and challenging but it can also be joyful, fulfilling and enlightening and for each person it is different.

Earlier this year I joined an art class run by Jan Sargeant (co-editor). Her wonderful encouragement and teaching persuaded me to paint for the first time in 30 years. In doing so, I learnt more about myself and I found a new angle entirely to how I really feel about this condition. Joining a class with other people living with Parkinson's gave me a perspective that I'd never even considered previously. I am therefore honoured to have been invited by Jennifer Yates and Jan Sargeant (editors) to write a preface to this book written by people living with and caring for those with the condition.

"Jigsaw" represents a small part of the Parkinson's community but its contributors hope that this small piece will link to others waging a battle with the disease; and piece by piece we will add to a more satisfying outcome for all of us. If "Jigsaw" can bring out just a small part of the artists and writers stories for you, then your experience will be both enlightening and emotional.

Thank you to all involved in this project for dedicating any profits to Parkinson's UK as we search for a cure and aim to support all people living with Parkinson's – both those diagnosed and their loved ones. Together we can make a difference and together we will.

GARY SHAUGNESSY
Gshaug7741@aol.com
Chair of Trustees, Parkinson's UK
May 2020

YOUR VOICE

We noble few,
we poets new,
don't stop your writing;
I'm inviting you to play.
A verse today is welcome
here on safe ground,
spread your words around
in such a way that says
you don't need to obey
archaic rules of grammar and metre.
There's nothing sweeter
than a poem from the soul;
to give your best,
you've passed any test
that matters.
The world's not flat,
remember that and turn
with confidence.
It's your choice,
it's your voice
we want to hear it.

JENNIFER YATES

TO A CARER

Look at me, look hard.
I mirror your fears,
your grief, your loss,
that gnawing need to understand
and raw, biting anger stabbing at you,
shouting "it's not fair".

Look at me again,
grieve for the future we had planned
then lost in a room full of people's tears
immune to pain,
glossy charts papered over
creeping cracks of disbelief.

Look at me harder,
avoid the guilt we see in the eyes we meet,
dance lightly in fear of breaking the eggs
as we tread on each other's dreams.
Hum softly a tune you never knew,
because we never wanted this.

But stop, and stay a moment in the now,
look again into the eyes,
reach out to touch that familiar hand
stroke the skin you've long known in love.
So when we look beyond what we each fear,
we are the same as ever we were, my dear.

JAN SARGEANT

THE FOUR SEASONS

Spring throws you into turmoil
clasping at your hand, and clawing at your arm,
from a deep dark rooted earthen splayed
tangle of knotted tubers and bulbs
thrusting against the soil to weakly fondle
slivers of shaking sunlight.
Aching in anticipation of being touched
and awoken, snowdrops raise their faces
to the sun's offer of a brief kiss.

Summer sweeps in with a swagger,
a Mick Jagger thrust your hips provocation
that makes young men gasp in disapproval
and the old snigger in to their Horlicks.
Silver birches throw their long branches
over the roofs of garden sheds which
fade as washed out shades of Farrow and Ball.
Riots of roses clamber among honeysuckle
giggling their scent and pricking unwary hands
with malevolent thorns then
rain arrives with thunder and splatters windows
bringing warm spurts of relief before the season
turns on its side and snores in the torpor following
short lived thrusts of hot desire.

Autumn sniffs the air and smiles in
anticipation of bonfires and rotting leaves.
She shrugs off an unwanted green mantle,
wraps russet silk around her breasts
and a sliver of mahogany velvet
between her thighs,

then she looks you in the eyes,
and whispers a welcoming sigh
of promise as the lost breaths
of summer slowly fade away.

Winter traces frost fingers against your window,
scratches for you to let him in
from the cold and the dark;
dark unlit streets
where snowflakes weep against pavements
and winds hurry down alleyways,
pulling thick coats around
shivering shoulders.
Ice draws patterns of smudged kisses
in the windscreens of cars
and commuters scrape at memories of sunlit days
and dream of the fevered caress
of a hand on summer kissed skin.
open the window, let the cold frigid touch
of winter clasp your hand and tremble
at its seductive touch.

JAN SARGEANT

DARK RIVER

I have travelled
up a long &
twisting dark river
with only
glimmers of life
from a star here
from the moonlight
there blanketed
by dark heavy air
hear audible
disturbances of
man and animals
from each shore
left and right hear
bells ring hear
birds sing from
tree limbs above
my head feel the
movement of air
up my neck
across my back
and listen with
my heart & soul
for the silence
taught to me by
Buddha but will
reside quite
independently
inside of me.

AL FERBER

JIGSAW

PHOTOGRAPHY BY LES WILLIAMS

TREES

Together we stand, tall and strong
standing here for ages long.
Ancient splendour, modern times
to protect a world beneath the skies.

Seasons change, year by year,
we shed our leaves, small buds appear
unfurling natures perfect gifts
fresh and new, all spirits lift.

Fed by sun and sparkling rain,
arms outstretched to heal the pain.
Shimmering, shuddering, in dappled hush
to calm and soothe the day long rush.

Help slow the stressful pace of life,
a healing balm to lesson strife.
Here we stand for all to see
magical, mystical, heavenly trees.

DEBBIE WILLIAMS

CUCKOO

I woke to find the day had dawned
and every bird was singing.
I woke to feel the pain of life
and every nerve was ringing.
I wondered, as I lay in bed,
what the day'd be bringing.
cuk-coo-coo
coo coo
cuk-coo-coo
coo-coo
cuk-coo-coo
coo coo cuk.

And then the rain began to fall;
I felt some consternation.
It had been falling many miles
to reach its destination.
Had I, like rain, been in free-fall
since the day of my creation?
cuk-coo-coo
coo-coo
cuk-coo-coo
coo-coo
cuk-coo-coo
coo coo cuk

And like the raindrops soak the earth
to quench the thirst of bowers,
my end will be to fuse with earth
for nourishment of flowers.
Enjoy today, the dove declared,

enjoy the days and hours.
cuk-coo-coo
coo-coo
cuk-coo-coo
coo-coo
cuk-coo-coo
coo-coo-cuk.

JOY LLOYD

MOON GAZING

Light pulls shadows from neglected corners,
spreading moonbeams on pebbled walls,
seeping into crannies, highlighting rooftops tall,
angled like a mountain range
Moon pokes rudely through the trees;
a waning moon that gazes down
before it slips behind a cloud
and winks an eye at me.

Moon reflected on the water,
creates a precious sight
that shimmers, dips and falls
in images striated with its light.
Moon casts her magic
spell by spell,
with secrets she is keeping;
secrets that preceded man,
but offered him a greeting.

For Moon has seen the world evolve
her memories are many,
yet she delights on balmy nights
to keep her secrets hidden.
Her gilded frame, a welcome sight,
a gift that's gladly given.
She shares her light
to our delight
and maintains her place in heaven.

JENNIFER YATES

THEN THERE WERE THREE

There are three in this marriage,
you, me and Parkinson's.
It's no tragic
arrangement, but
a disaster.
For better or best,
worse is a test
of strength,
and feelings set reeling.
Another presence
revealing
exceptional emotions,
no notion
of where this is going;
not knowing
how things will end.

JENNIFER YATES

FABRIC – ATIONS

When thin layers of honesty
are woven as false truths,
justice weaves a heavy weft
of disbelief,
embroiders thin threads
amongst darkly velvet comfortable lies;
truth rolls over
whispers "enough",
gazes in fear at the space
between what was,
what is,
what might have been,
and laughs at itself.

JAN SARGEANT

THE BED I LONG TO CLIMB INTO

The bed I longed to climb into
has become a place of woe,
because I cannot sleep at night
yet I've nowhere else to go.
You try to stop me doing
all the things I loved to do,
you're like a tiny monster
that got watered and you grew
into this horrible being
that devours me bit by bit,
but soon we'll have an answer
and you will have to quit.
Quit your reign of terror,
that you impose on all of us;
for a cure will come eventually
then we will watch you crushed to dust.

CAROL BOWDEN

BUBBLES BEFORE BREAKFAST

Blow bubbles before breakfast
if troubles come your way,
blow bubbles before breakfast
and watch them float away.
If fear overwhelms you
in the middle of the night;
get up, blow gentle bubbles
all will be alright.
When the pain you have
is making you feel down,
get your tub of bubbles out
smile no need to frown.
If your world seems empty
and things don't go your way,
fill the sky with bubbles
to brighten up your day.
Blowing bubbles before breakfast
seems a childish thing to do,
but sometimes it's the little things
that help to see you through.

DEBBIE WILLIAMS

IT'S A BUGGER WHEN ………

It's a bugger when ……….

Words dance into mind
jumbletumble
onto page,
mumblingrumbling
stumblingfumbling
rummaging round
for the right one
the elusive one
hidden in the crease
between sleep and dream
taunting haunting
peekaboo possibilities,
a tantilising promise
lingering out of reach.

JAN SARGEANT

THE SELFLESS ACT OF GIVING

Generosity is giving
without a thought for self.
It is a way of living
independent of one's wealth.
It's in a person's nature,
her attitude to life;
it's something we can nurture
as we battle through this life.
It's a smile to passing strangers
it's a 'Thank You' truly meant.
It's the step you take
to celebrate
the birthday of a friend.
It's remembering the sadness
of loss in people's lives;
a loving touch that comforts
on which friendship relies.
And when you're feeling lonely,
isolated too,
It's the message in your inbox
that matters so to you.
It takes generosity of spirit
to think of others' plight,
but it's worth the effort you put in
that makes me feel alright.
It's a challenge 'mid the chaos
of a pandemic spread,
to give not take and educate,
to lead and not be led.
It's a selfless act of kindness,
it's a universal truth,

that somehow, will remind us
and help to pull us through.

JENNIFER YATES

I REALLY DIDN'T WANT YOU

I really didn't want you,
I never asked you in
you snuck up very quietly,
before I knew you were him.

The one who makes me shiver
then tremble like its cold
who makes me shuffle, stoop and fall
and generally feel old.

You give me so much trouble,
you are a total pest
but I'll get by with humour
plus a warm and cosy vest!

My fingers can't pick up my change,
the cashiers sigh and mutter,
the customers who stand in line
can't understand my stutter.

The words won't come, the hands won't work,
the brain, it's at a standstill.
Then movement starts I can't control
like I'm dancing to a band – brill!

The cramps that curl my toes at night
then travel up my leg,
they creep up to my shoulder
and stop me turning in my bed.

My skin it flakes upon my nose,
how it makes me feel so scaly;
the urge to use the loo at once,
what now? Urgently? Yes really!!

But wait I have my trusty meds
that mix of patch and pill;
I might not be invincible
but they help me climb that hill.

The one that I look down from
to see people far worse off than me,
to know that I'll survive this
and that I will stay free.

You will not beat me Parkinson's,
I will not let you win,
for I am strong in thought and know
you're fit only for the bin.

CAROL BOWDEN

SILLY O'CLOCK

It's half past silly o'clock
in the morning,
all I want to do is sleep.
I lay here tossing and turning,
I've lost count of how many fillipin' sheep
are skipping around the room.
All I want to do is sleep.
I put on some pretty music,
they say it is calming and soothing,
but I tell you now, if I don't get some sleep,
it's my mind I will be losing.
I am still awake at silly o'clock
in the early hours of the morning.
I lie here trying to relax
and stop the incessant yawning.
All I want is some sleep.
So off I go to make a warm drink
making more noise trying to be quiet
as the spoon clatters in the sink.
The 'not hot' cross buns look oh, so very tempting;
ah well, tomorrow I'll start my diet
and back to bed I go.
Then ouch! I stub my effing toe.
I'm still awake at silly o'clock
please, all I want is some sleep.
The new day is dawning
and the blessed birds begin to cheep!
I cannot believe it is already nearly morning.
all I want is some flipping sleep!

KAREN BROWNE

CHEESE ON TOAST

Oh, for some cheese on toast,
it doesn't matter which type, brie, blue, mild cheddar,
    mature cheddar
or any other smelly cheese with walnuts or raisins or
    cranberries,
I don't mind, how about you?

Whether it's on cut loaf, brown loaf or gluten free
I'm really not fussy, it's only our tea
not tea and cakes or any fancy bakes
or anything Mr Kipling makes;
its just cheese on toast,
that's what I miss most, that melting moment
and the smell of cheese that melts me heart and wobbles
    me knees,
and makes me sneeze,
more cheese please, it melts with ease, I'll 'ave more
    please.

For it stands the test of time and goes down well without
    a smell,
it burns the tongue and then – the yell!
But who can tell that burnt toast smell
sadly, yours to eat and not yet mine.

COLIN PIDGLEY

THE LIFE OF AN ADMINISTRATOR

The life of an administrator is very strange,
they live in a cupboard
and swim out of drains.
Their eight eyes gleam bright
as they sweep over a page,
looking for what?
They're not sure, but they gauge
the responses to posts
that members have made,
at the same time declining persons
who fell short of the grade
required for membership of the group.
Simple questions to answer,
no need to jump through a hoop.
Though you wouldn't think it
when reading replies that are written
bear no resemblance to questions
however they're given,
but safety of members
is always their aim.
So whilst off site they joke and act silly,
they care for their members,
the group and each other.
In fact it's like spending a week
with your mother.

CAROL BOWDEN

KIDS TODAY

Interaction
pure distraction
total loss of satisfaction
kids on WIFI, parents too
eyes on screens like super glue.
Pepper Pig and You Tube mix
kids on Wotsits fatty snack
parental conversation lack
it's how we live in pure illusion
these times of digital revolution.

BARRY WIGGINS

BRITISH JUSTICE

Sal said it weren't her what did it,
set fire to the clouds,
took a flame to the thrower,
she swore on the Bible she'd never read,
to tell a truth never believed in,
still less recognised,
and smiled winningly across the room,
without showing the broken tooth,
a prize from the last fight she'd had

No, she swore, she didn't stand back
and watch as the blaze reached ever upwards,
scouring the darkness with orange,
she preferred red, she said.
Weren't her, couldn't be.
She'd been shopping.

The jury looked,
strained skirt, borrowed jacket,
badly rimmed lips around a fag lined mouth,
the legal aid in worn out suit
shiny with disbelief.
Found her guilty.
Right verdict.
wrong reasons.

JAN SARGEANT

MR PARKINSON'S

So we start the dance
Parkinson's begins to call
with twitch and quiver
hand and foot
running freestyle action
beating it's own drum.
never a set tempo
the silent conductor
never a sound
but action speaks forth
others nod towards me
druggy or a drunk is the assumption
an instant verdict concludes call.

BARRY WIGGINS

THE GHOST SHIP

Between the tip of the mast and the keel of the hull,
then the lull of the sloop from the port to starboard waves
the tiller dances side to side as if conducting an
      orchestra,
the dagger board raised is cleared so slightly by the swing
      of the boom,
whilst a loose and wayward block beats on the chock as it
      grips the stern.
Like a mini brigantine she sat and rocked and failed to lie
unlike her older sister, who was left and found,
by the Grace of God so long ago.
With 'Every sail set, the tiller lashed fast, not a rope was
      out of place' and yet
this was the modern lost and lonely, new aged,
      millennium Mary Celeste.

BARRY WIGGINS

PC

PC took on a new meaning
when it stopped worrying
about being politically correct,
didn't care if it was gender blind,
gender neutral,
gender undecided
or non gendered,
a neologism awaiting recognition
in its own acronym
on a toilet door.

PC became pre Corona,
post Corona, peri Corona
a covid of logarithmic importance,
the new sine and cosine
with 19 as Pi
the isosceles triangle
a motif for isolation,
quadratic equations banned
in favour of factions and
socially distanced units –
at which tangentital point
the circle was finally squared.

JAN SARGEANT

PHOTOGRAPH BY MIKE YATES

CASTLE URQUHART

Urquhart stands bleak and severe
like a rotting tooth, here
clinging to the shore, a kiss planted, a caress
on the gaping mouth that is Loch Ness.

Centuries of aging blew around this shore,
whispering rumours of battle and more.
Keeping the castle out of their reach,
impenetrable walls that cannot be breached.

Battle sore warriors defending their home,
while enemy soldiers are chilled to the bone.
Then a monster is woken from a deep sleep
she stirs in the waters deeper than deep.

She rises, then dives, a legend revealed
but she is elusive, a shadow sealed
in dark waters deep in the Loch
her nest made up of pieces of rock.

Yet that brief sighting is enough to engage
the fear of the enemy frozen in rage.
The battle for Urquhart is over and won,
thanks to the monster who caused them to run.

The monster now sleeping, basks in the deep
defending the castle, it's secret to keep.
Yet the monster's a legend, one that persists,
while the castle's a symbol that truly exists.

Urquhart's been here for hundreds of years
it stands as a symbol of blood, sweat and tears.
It highlights a time when battles were rife
and stands as a lesson in defending your life.

JENNIFER YATES

HANDBAGS ON NOSES

Handbags on noses
and biscuits in mittens
dull painted chickens in corners are sitting
tiny banana skins ready to fling
just a few 'dafties' to make us all sing.
When the door shuts
when the car stalls
when I'm feeling bad,
I simply dismember my flowering bush
because YES, I am quite mad.

BARRY WIGGINS

WHEN ROBOTS START TO DIE

Warning, warning
late at night
power loss
no strength to light
illumination void
memory loss I'm so annoyed.
Danger, danger almost flat
file save routines where it's at
data dumps and sub routines race
all for one the final chase
must finish, end of day
lines of code begin to stray
another robot gone awry.

BARRY WIGGINS

LOVE LETTERS

Words interest me
a lot.
It's not that they have letters
or a full stop.
It's not the cursive nature
of their form,
it's how they adorn
the page
bringing to life,
forging a meaning
into a sentence,
makes sense to me.
I can see
the way words paint pictures,
like those of Michelangelo.
Brave words, holy words,
words with no purpose
that hide secrecy.
Wording not timed,
written in script
or printed,
I don't mind.
They stimulate my brain;
write to me again.
I'll treasure
forever,
the words, that you write.

JENNIFER YATES

WORDS

I like words when they
      spill
over, crash onto the page
urgencyscribbled letters
scramble for shape
demand to be heard
abandon themselves
wanton words
wanting words
wooing words
words to coax, words to hurt,
words about words
lined up typed up messed up
washed up, fucked up,
words scrawled across skies
vapour trails which fade
handprints lost in sand

I like words,
I don't trust them.

JAN SARGEANT

MY DAILY BATTLE

My daily battle with Parkinson's
is like flying a kite on the breeze,
soaring so high …. plummeting low
just like the tide, the ebb and the flow.

Parkinson's changes cognition.
It's progressive, degenerative,
a neurological condition.
It robs you of speech and blurs your vision.

People make comments,
I scowl as they mutter
"You don't look ill,
is your Parkinson's better?"

It will not improve,
there's no pill to remove.
I'll not get better for sure
but in time, there will be a cure.

ANDY CLEGG

WEARING THE RED ROSE

Wearing the Red Rose
standing tall and proud
brotherhood
side by side
fifteen players as one nation
ruck and maul
focus and dig deep
eighty minutes to live or die,
a nation holds its breath
anthem sung with pride:
game on.

BARRY WIGGINS

36   JIGSAW

HOLD MY HAND

Hold my hand
come sit with me and hold my hand,
let's remember all we did
when we were young and carefree
before we knew that he had hid.

Hid inside me, lurking
taking time to grow
till he decided to emerge
and put himself on show.

Taking all my memories
shredding them to dust
making visions come to life,
to scare me if they must.

Causing me to feel a fool
as I stumble over words,
freezing me so I can't walk
then producing so much drool.

Laughing at me always
as I try to get undressed,
mocking my inability
to cope with all the stress.

He tries to stop me doing
all the things that I had planned,
but I'll fight on determined
as long as you can hold my hand.

CAROL BOWDEN

TELL THE TRUTH

Tell the truth……..
when you write words on a page,
when your words breathe with life
when they pulse with an image,
play the heartbeat of a sound
in a line which doesn't scan
a line that has no rhyme,
is there a point at which
you feel the ache of a syllable
deep inside your belly
a metaphorical gash
through sculpted stanzas
behind which you hide

your real fears.

JAN SARGEANT

PARKINSON'S

You are shaking and I press closer
to share discomfort
or to reassure myself – I cannot tell.
Reassure ... was there ever full assurance
and can there be
when separated into two minds?
Are we together here, now,
in this quaking bed.
As one lies still, thinking
and the other tries to?

Like a rubber band wound up and then released,
twists
so your traitor limbs tantrum
and we wait
for the unwinding.
We coexist
you, wanting me to be oblivious,
me, wanting to climb into you and share
all.

JOY LLOYD

PHOTOGRAPH BY BARRY WIGGINS

SEED HEAD

One dandelion seed head
hurled across skies
a thousand universes
windwhipped through trees
laughing through a cold breeze
as millions of planets
whirl around new suns
moonrays pierce night stars
warm lips touch waves
make them smile
tides groan and moan
with desire
as they straddle sands

A dandelion bursts,
and a zillion doors
open wide,
beckon to you, call to you
dare you step inside.

JAN SARGEANT

AFTER THE RAIN

The sky is on the ground
outside,
looking deeper than sleep.
A bird swims in the depths
wings wide
tipped-up-side-down.
Lights twink-shrink in dull sun.
A worm
writhes larger than trees
caught up in a cloud
high – high
it storm-stirs as it dies.
Infinity fell splash
mashed mid
dashed in splinters of wet.
It glimmers grounded.
The deep
sweeps shallow for wading.
Step into the heavens
and stamp
with rage for goodness sake.
Make skies crash-flash
to soak
your socks damp to your thighs.

JOY LLOYD

CHAMELEON

It's just a different kind of wonderful,
chasing old rainbows up darkened streets
won't get you to a new destination.
Take a breath, stand still, look around you,
then dive in to the clouds and raise your fist in salute
as you swoop and soar and laugh in the cold spurts of
new life grinning in your face and shouting come on then.
Find undisclosed paths through forests of discovery
change the compass and set it to south not north.
Why not. It's your compass.
Take the battery out of the old radio,
re-tune the wavelength and set your sights
on the heart of the moon.
Choose to hear a different tune.
Why not. It's your melody.
Look in a new direction, take the pin out of the map,
throw aside your expectations
and see what comes of that.
It's just a different kind of wonderful.

JAN SARGEANT

AUTUMN

Autumn colours in all their glory,
announce the beauty, the memories, the story
of ancient trees in woodland scene,
of times gone by,
times not yet been,
carpet of leaves caress the ground;
new fallen splendour,
softly whispered sound.

DEBBIE WILLIAMS

ON AFRICAN PLAINS

I am an eagle
soaring majestically,
hunting down my prey.

I am a lion.
The alpha male,
on African plains, I rule.

I am a bull elephant,
leader of the herd:
for miles my trumpeting is heard.

I am a wildebeest
and I am the prey,
hoping to make through the day ….

I usually do!

ANDY CLEGG

MR PD

Who or what are you, Mr PD
to invade my body
with this horrible disease.
I shake, I ache,
I stumble, not fall,
I slur and I dribble,
I'm not happy at all.

Do I walk down the road
with my head held high?
No I shuffle along, head always down,
shaking and stumbling
my face, in a permanent frown.
I've walked a little, my house still in sight,
I need to go back,
so I'm in for a fight.

A challenge, a chore, I'm finally home,
my feet, legs and body
are all feeling sore.
No-one knows what Mr PD
has done to me;
I used to be lively,
witty, quite pretty
so I've been told.

But since this disease
has invaded my brain
I feel as if I'm going insane.
I'm miserable, morbid, angry, tearful,
fearful of how much worse it will get.

I haven't lived my life yet!
Now please leave my body.

So Mr PD, take a ticket to Mars
then I amongst others,
can thank our lucky stars.
Then, when we are out and about,
we can look to the sky,
Our glasses held high;
and make a toast to old Parky:
"up yours and bye bye!"

HAZEL MORGAN

PALINDROME

Like a well worn record
the needle hits the groove
around it spins off kilter
again and again it undulates
the quick action lunges into motion
from off to on it begins.
The quick action lunges into motion
again and again it undulates
around it spins off kilter
the needle hits the groove
like a well worn record.

BARRY WIGGINS

PILLOWS AND PILLS

The darkness yawns its time for bed
as bright lights shine upon my head.
Get up, get up,
I heard them say,
it's time to start a brand new day.

I'd rather be sleeping,
it's silly o'clock,
the sound of a tick, then a tock.
In the distance upon the trees
the sound of birds' sweet melodies.

With eyes now open
the morning broken
shutters opened across the land.
I survey what's mine and all is well,
all that's missing is my sense of smell.

It's time now to take those meds,
the ones they said would fix our heads.
Green and purple,
there's red, white and blue
but the more I take the more I need to

Now finally it's done,
let's start the day
and have some fun.
The sun comes out to kiss the day;
I've said my piece, I'm on my way ....

COLIN PIDGLEY

PRACTISING THE FORM

Stand in Wu Chi
knees slightly bent,
clear your mind of intent.

BREATHE

Left leg steps one stride
sideways.
Sink through the knees,
focus and

BREATHE

Parallel arms raise
then lower, pushing down
on an invisible cloud
that takes your thoughts
away from the present.

BREATHE

..... into the form,
your body knows the way,
no need to remember,
rely on muscle memory
and .....

BREATHE

A wave of movement
we move as one body
through 'cloud hands',
'monkey steps back'
watching the dance.

BREATHE

Movement flows
to a close,
left foot meets right,
stand upright
and

BREATHE

The form is complete,
repeat whenever
you need
to calm your mind.
Take a tip from me and

BREATHE.

JENNIFER YATES

THE MOMENT

Light filters through a rusty shaded tree-line
deep, deep sea of hues and shapes
greens and browns dot scarcely here and there
out in the void, a cuckoo calls,
it's vocal hoot a cry of the jester,
whilst thin brown gnarled finger-like tree trunks
dive into sodden soil
another fool burn into the scam of responsibility.
A fool of love and caring and the tricksters we meet
light shoots a beam of laser-like pointer across the floor,
where water laid puddles and droplets of water,
pass on the light like a diamond encrusted
cloak to walk upon like a spiritual carpet.
Then you see train lines,
are they coming or going,
are we on a journey or are we there?
When did it start or stop?
life is a spiritual mystery
paths wind and twist ahead and behind.
We toil and ponder on right or wrong BUT
miss the very answer, a simple one we are often blind to see
ask not the pathway, the journey's route,
the question of am I going here or there,
have I begun, arrived or started
because you are here, you are in the moment,
....................always.

BARRY WIGGINS

THE IRON HORSE.

The Iron Horse came to a hill,
a climb to make by metal rail stood on rock and shale.
Hewn by men and beast in sweat and blood,
a task it could not, would not fail.
Each empty cart hooked then filled,
the load it carries for the good;
this man-made beast was brought to life, but has no
      mortal soul.
It's scratching noise like voice, as if the Devil's harp
calls out loud across the valley and the vale
built for burden,
its huge black side all sleek and sharp;
hard raised rivets welded to the frame, to hold the beast
      intact.
No need to sleep or rest, it has a fiery heart of coal
that beats each piston out and in, with relentless motion
      moving further on,
as inch by inch, it finds the summit and backs off to carry
      on
until it comes again.

BARRY WIGGINS

PAINT ME A POEM

She paints pictures with a pen,
draws words into a scene,
carefully places strides of colour
blended to meet lines on the page.
Letters tinged with light
fading to full stops
capture the imagination
in a landscape of letters.
Spreading words across a canvas
where colours run in rainbow notes
bring joy to a reader
who, with fresh eyes
completes the picture.
The depth of meaning in the scene
dawns as final brush strokes blend,
and only she can sense
what the writer intends.
Her reader becomes the one
who embellishes the whole
and draws it to her soul.

JENNIFER YATES

GROWING OLDER WITH PARKINSON'S

When I grow old no Parky purple for me,
drains the face of colour, darling.
No I think a perfectly respectable shade of off white,
off pink, off blue, off anything,
nothing too dramatic.
And never a red hat, my dear, far too obvious.
I shan't be rattling any railings with my stick,
nor spitting in any gardens, how gross.
No, I shall wear yellow
with a nauseous shade of green shoes
and cover myself in acrylic paint
and tell people I'm an artist.
I shall serve soups made with lentils and bugger all else
and pretend I'm vegan, just for the laugh of it,
and to see the horror on people's faces
when you tell them you're allergic to Aldi's wines.
When I grow old, my mischief will be boundless
as a child's and my playground will be life.
And the greatest thrill of all, my dear,
put your teeth back in to smile …….
I'm already there.

JAN SARGEANT

FIELD OF DREAMS

In my field of dreams
I plant the seeds of thoughts
to where there is always sunshine in the rain.
The water that runs down my cheek is of joy, not pain
when the glass is half empty but your heart is almost full,
your love is going nowhere and the door to life seems dull.
So you stub love out like a cigarette, half smoked in the
      doorway to your soul;
the hopes and fears collude up to sort your karmic goal,
and as you reach to hold the hand of someone you love,
who understands as feelings back inside your core
to make it feel it was always so planned.
You wipe a tear off your face
then brush your hair back into place
and find a smile to last you all the week
that brings happiness to your face,
whilst all is good, the bad in part
could drive a stake into your heart;
now rest your face on pillows soft and cool
whilst sadness, plays its part

BARRY WIGGINS.

NO GOING BACK

Before the snow painted branches
in feathered white layers,
before the snow sang its soft shushing song
into the silence of a listening night,
I did, you know I did.

When the rain splattered hard,
drowning youth's frail hopes
with harsh threats of reality,
you accepted what was offered.
You did, you know you did.

After storm clouds fragment into
bitter memories of broken pasts,
the memory of what once was there
echoes through empty corridors.
And you're lost, you know you're lost.

As the sad song shuffles a silent requiem
through dusty rooms filled with regrets,
the walls you built in anger that day
sob softly in sorrow at what you did.
What you did, what you know you did.

And the walls whisper back
what you already knew,
There's no going back now,
Never again,
not for you.

JAN SARGEANT

PAINTING BY TED KENNEDY

INVISIBLE LIGHT

It caught me by surprise
your painting;
as my eyes scanned the image,
I drank in the pinks and cerulean blue.
My ears caught the scream of gulls,
salt soaked screeching
wheeling, reeling,
pecking at my brain,
hiding behind tumbling rain
as if to pull my attention.

In that moment
when I saw it
I had to possess the painting.
It spoke to me in a thousand tongues.
Colour blending, a nerve sending
shivers down my spine,
seascape pulls me in,
I feel the breeze on my skin,
the sun on my face
see the horizon through the haze.
A chimera of light at sunset,
waves receding, slowly leaving
the shore; colour eclipses my mind.
Memories, I find, invoked,
Provoked to find
solace of a kind,
in Invisible Light.

JENNIFER YATES

NO PARTY

It's no party
living with Parky.
Tremor increasing,
now I'm keeping
appointments with clinicians,
but nobody listens
to how, I am feeling.

Writing, once a pleasure
words are now minuscule
and I'm the fool
who can't read what she's written.
I'm the one bitten
by this disease.
No ease.

Every day there is pain,
walking's not the same;
I fight to rise from my chair,
it's a struggle to keep
food on my fork.
Wearing a pinny
in case I spill any.

It's so demeaning
this feeling
of inability,
of disability,
increasing in need
still trying to succeed.

Feeling
the strain.
Anxiety creeping,
slowly increasing,
ruling my life.
Can't cope with tomorrow,
these feelings of sorrow.
It's no party
living with Parky.

JENNIFER YATES

THE RHYTHM OF LIFE

Seconds tick as tides swell and shift across sands
lined by seconds ticking
as tides swell and shift across
Sands which yield but never surrender,
timeless echoes of tides which swell;
leaving rivulets of water glistening
in screams of betrayal at being left behind,
their tears a sad reminder that life was once there.
The water trickles against sad sand
and strokes its gentle caress of hope.

Seconds tick by and new tides swell
and shift across sands erasing old lines,
creating new ones
swelling the music and beating a drum
in time with time.

The face that smiled behind the rocks
was etched in lines of laughter and shared pain.
Words jumbled hopscotch of hops and stops
and chalk pieces thrown down along the way,
a lifetime of promises and secrets shared
wanting so much to be heard.

The sands shudder in the trembling light,
a new day, a new tide. The boats glide out across
silver waters and tease the dawn
with their quiet ripples and the splash splash of
waves against bark.

I am the tide that touches your breath
against a lifetime of breaths
and feels you roar in agony
as life pulls you back.

Seconds tick as tides swell
and shift across sands
for always.

JAN SARGEANT

A STEP TOO FAR

I forget the connection between lies and deception,
Sweet Columbine whispers to grey cats in gutters;
where hags circle a bubbling cauldron
and fair Juliet lolls about on her balcony
whispering disjointed phrases of where not why.
For ages she's been moping,
thinking of eloping with a lad called Romeo.
Juliet calls his name,
but would it sound the same
if his name was Bryan?
Juliet thinks, oh hang it;
the parents are against the pairing.
She considers Bryan, gone off with colourful friends;
perhaps he'll change direction (or his name)
follow Titania's example and find love
in the eyes of a dumb creature.
Meanwhile Romeo's gone around the world with Puck,
oh f*** flipping heck, he's giving her the elbow!
Juliet almost drags herself over the balcony.
It's too dramatic,
yet Juliet resolves to attract attention
and swallows poison
a step too far!

That balcony was never strong enough
to hold the passions of a Romeo.
Shakespeare nailed it with 'sweet sorrow'
no worries, there's always tomorrow
which leads on a petty pace.

JENNIFER YATES

DOPAMINE BLUES

No dopamine today
the prescription's gone astray;
requested in mid April
and now we're into May.
I could see where this was going
'cos I didn't get the message
saying 'medication coming'.
So a second request went out,
I assumed that there was doubt,
or the surgery under-manned;
things don't always go to plan.
There's corona to consider,
causing everyone to dither,
so I can understand
if my request was in a queue
and I was just one of the few
who were thankful just to be
Corona virus free.
But as my tablets reduced in number
and I was forced to go without,
I realised the value
of that little blue capsule.
So today I am hoping
the postman will deliver
the levadopa I am missing,
meanwhile I feel the tremor
of the Dopamine Blues.

JENNIFER YATES

BAGGAGE COLLECTORS

They collect the detritus
from other people's lives,
sniff it,
taste it,
touch it,
know why it wasn't wanted
in the first place.

Baggage collectors unpack
other people's lies, absorb
and absolve as if bestowing
a blessing of penitence.
They walk the road others have chosen,
too afraid to choose their own,
they grasp at bags they never packed,
never theirs, clutch at someone's life
knowing theirs lacked,
had been empty
for some time in fact.

JAN SARGEANT

DYSNOMIA

There's a tiger in my soup,
the man cried:
get it out, get it out!
I don't believe it should be there,
people stare.
is it because I'm dreaming?
Are they scheming,
all those people
nameless, shameless,
shouting.

The waiter pulls up a chair,
I'm standing
demanding to speak to the maitre'd.
Who cares?
They stare and mumble,
grumble.
I'm not intoxicated,
not high on Charlie.
I'm agitated, why?

When did a tiger become a fly?

JENNIFER YATES

LOST SENSE

I cannot smell the honeysuckle,
I cannot smell the rose,
I think that Parkinson's Disease did
Something to my nose.

I cannot smell the bonfire
Or the smoke that's in my hair.
I'm wondering just what else I'll lose,
I guess it isn't fair.

I cannot smell the new mown lawn
Or soft refreshing rain.
I'm wondering if it's gone for good
Or will return again.

And even though it's simple
Just to lose your sense of smell,
It's those subtle, little changes
That creep up on you so well.

But I can smell your perfume,
Though it's in my memory;
It's part of just accepting
What is happening to me.

SALLY CHURCH

THE PAINTER

As the painter sits
the canvas stretches over wood,
like the beginning of a new day
with flow and ease and gentle strokes,
just like the dawn of sunrise
greets a new day.

The painter reaches for his palette;
golden sunshine bringing memories
where gentle waves roll in and out
like diamonds dancing gently across the sea
and sweet salt air whispers through the breeze.

Now with flowing ease,
the painter picks up his brush
as silent colours wait
to see which ones he'll choose.
The flowing motion of the paint
lands like birds at sea,
like sandcastles on the sand.

And the sounds of laughter
of times gone by.

COLIN PIDGLEY

A TRIAD OF DRAGONS:

1. Fear: Blue Dragons
Blue dragons find the fear inside;
breathe frosty flames of dread
over, and around my head.
My mind seeks salvation,
yet denied,
it fails to find a place to hide.

Blue dragons search in corners of my mind;
blue flames lick the sides of my fear
and gather tributaries of molten stress,
spilling it carelessly over vivid imagination,
sublimely spread
in their consternation.

Blue dragons seek out a place to feed,
find nightmares locked inside
and gorge themselves without remorse.
They remain,
and laconically
they torture me ...
of course.

2. Fight: Red Dragons
Red dragons unseen
hide in storm clouds,
rest, on flights of fancy
breathing their flares,
and igniting the air
with molten spurs:
reaching their target.

PAINTING BY JAN SARGEANT

Red dragons take flight
in a display of might:
one glance from their eyes
sends shockwaves through skies,
as the dragons smite,
flaming arrows slice sight:
and the storm wrecks all in it's wake.

Red dragons wait
until fading light,
their thunderous movement curtailed.
No seeking of treasure
but measure for measure,
red dragons' pleasure;
assembling, the souls of the dead.

3. Free: Green Dragons
Green dragons are found
in locations remote,
inaccessibly tucked away.
In small groups they remain,
stoically the same,
green dragons are
unchanged.

Green dragons are free,
they practice Tai Chi,
meditating daily.
A mantra for peace
they continuously repeat;
for green dragons
there's hope in the moment.

Green dragons hold a power
deeper than deep;
a place only they recognise.
Whilst we are asleep,
green dragons creep
and place their love
in your heart.

JENNIFER YATES

MY DEAR

Your face is not frozen as you fear;
I can read what it tells me still.
Your hand may shake,
your leg may quake
but these movements are precious to me, my dear,
yes your movements are precious to me.

Our love is not leaving as you fear,
I will love you forever still.
I'd not exchange,
if you derange
for your moments are worth all to me, my dear,
yes your moments are worth all to me.

Your life is not lessened as you fear,
there is lots of enjoyment still.
The worst can't come,
till the best is done –
our best is not done even half, my dear,
and you still are the one for me

JOY LLOYD

THE ARTIST

When you before me,
in a tumbled light
paint pictures boldly
with bright brush strokes
that express all the elements
of wasted years.
Giving glimpses of a haunted face,
notions of seasick waves,
I can discern, between the clouds
of mist filled folds;
those peeping eyes,
now troubled, hold me
in a captivating smile,
just like La Gioconda
plain and staring
with someone else's eyes.

JENNIFER YATES

A POINT AT THE END

There's a point at the end of the line,
where anything could happen,
your friend, the one who paints music,
he said the train stops here,
so you step down,
look at baggage grabbed
from a memory ago,
leave it in lost property,
throw away the ticket,
dance through the barrier,
breathe the fresh air
of whatever
wherever
whenever

It was an open ticket
with no return.

JAN SARGEANT

JIGSAW PUZZLE

Statement: Jigsaw pieces scattered
hide a picture of my life,
some fit easily together
matching colour,
matching size,
linking in with the same contours
shapes that mirror, in relief;
fit together, there was pleasure
in the whole you used to see.

I am like that jigsaw puzzle,
I don't fold, yet now I crease,
and my edges don't define
what's going on inside my mind.
I may not fit together
as once I used to be,
but below the jumbled surface
there's a glimmer
of the girl I used to be.

Response: scattered pieces of your life
huddle with the shifting shapes
and fragments of another's,
a minglemix of minds
playing word games on a page
we hear each other's silent cries
feel the contours of each other's sighs.

I have measured out my life
in the fractured possibilities
of potential paths and ways ahead

in the sudden dead ends of lies
I'm a Rubrik cube with no corners,
An enigma without instruction
A pattern with no construction

Place the pieces down wherever you will
The shadows of what we were are there still.

Can you see us?

JAN SARGEANT & JENNIFER YATES

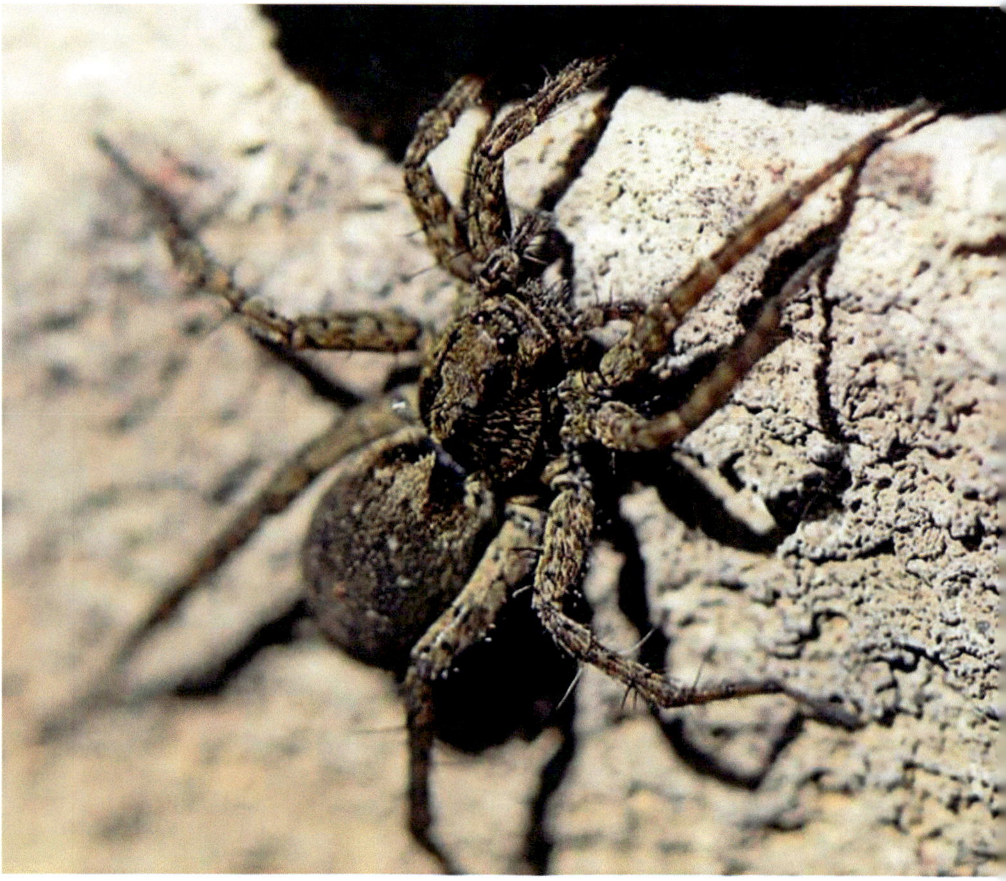

WEB SPINNERS

Spinning silk cobwebs, she twists
gently pulling at the floundering fool.
The spider shrugs into the Autumn morning
letting woven silk threads shimmer.
Dew drops gather on precious lace
adding sparkle to a night's labour.
Languorous legs untangle themselves from rotted leaves.
She feels heavy with desire, clotted with hunger.
A bleary eyed moth staggers into the sticky curtain,
flaps tired wings; a useless effort, a welcome meal.
'So long sucker' mouths the spider threading its way
to the certainty of one always willing to wait.
Miss Muffet interjected with her curds and whey,
teased the spider, who perched
on a convenient snail, mouthed expletives.
'Not sure about the ending' said the tuffet,
'I was always there for you.'

JAN SARGEANT & JENNIFER YATES

THE PAINTING: POSSESSION OR POSSESSOR

Question: Can you possess a painting?

Sure, you can buy and own the canvas,
you can hang it on your wall,
you can show it off or hide it away
stroke it, touch it, revere it each day
you can slice it, shred it,
do what you want to, eh,
it's yours when you pay .....

but what was it that guided the hand
that made the marks,
that brushed the strokes,
that chose the palette
smoothed shadows across seas
screeched seagulls with a black dot
smashed waves on ochre sand
which shimmer under apricot moons,
sting your eyes with salt spray
and leave lips dried by the wind

The painting possesses the painting,
and it owns you
as you stare.

Answer: To possess is to behold
with eyes blinded by tears.
The canvas holds a message
for one who knows its worth.
But words are purely tokens

we exchange for etiquette's sake,
yet a painting speaks in colour
and it does not dictate.
It instantly connects
with someone who is listening
and with eyes that can't forget,
the painting.

JAN SARGEANT & JENNIFER YATES

CLIFFHANGER

Voice: One day
a rock chiselled its way
out of the cliff,
laughing.
Danced naked into the abyss,
and when it got to the bottom
of a long, long dark drop,
I knew there was no going back.

Regret is
self – indulgence.
Lesson – stop chiselling.

Echo: Regret is fruitless,
useless,
a barrier to growth.
Its unbecoming
to strum a useless tune.
Braver by far
to follow your star
meeting your shadow
face on
takes fortitude
I'm not being rude
but get a grip,
act quick,
to distil the myth
and pack that chisel
slap bang in the middle
and let Cliff address
the problem of division.

Voice: Cliff sounds like a singer I can't stand.

JIGSAW

Echo: Cliff or cliff,
what the heck!
I took the bother
to include Shadows
in my rhyme.
Cliffs will tumble in time
yet words will linger
whoever the singer,
your choice, not mine.

Voice: Cliff crumbled
under the weight of
Beatles burrowing into
the lives of pubescent girls
who grew up to throw their knickers
onto a stage which
contained neither a Cliff nor a Beatle.
Fickle fans.
Elles ne regrettes rein.
Edith picked up the chisel
and began again
as the life model shivered
in his blue suede shoes.

Echo: More power to Piaf's elbow
a woman with no regrets.
Cliff defeated
Beatles cheated
Elvis, not to my taste.
I rest my case
or should that be
completed?

JAN SARGEANT & JENNIFER YATES

PINK HARES AND OTHER DREAMS

Thinking cap on a slumbering head,
a useless invitation
which laughed as it slid to the floor
meeting reluctant eyes with scorn.

Upstaged, the cap slumbers on
in anticipation of a fun-filled afternoon,
which arrived …. in the form of a pink, full toothed hare,
about three o'clock, clutching a bottle of cheap plonk.

The hare, being of sound mind and a firm limbed body
looked around before saluting his hostess
and running away with his own cap
jauntily placed on his woolly head.
But too late, the hare hesitated, and in that moment
the thinking cap roused the slumbering body with a nudge.

The hazy dawn seeped through silent walls
pushing pink hare dreams out of the window.
Arms slowly numbing back into life
rubbing movement back into stone legs,
a yawn leaves trembling lips
and settles forlornly on stupefied reflections
mirrored in a lover's gaze.

JAN SARGEANT & JENNIFER YATES

MEET THE POETS

CAROL BOWDEN
A Lancashire Lass by birth, I've lived in Cheshire for most of my life. I've never considered myself a poet before but now I can say I'm a poet with Parkinson's. I never really understood the nuances of poetry; to me poetry should rhyme, perhaps I'm a bit of a Philistine in my views. For me poetry is fun but I have to confess, I do possess a book of Indian Love Poems which I adore.

KAREN BROWNE
I am a complete newcomer to writing, especially poetry. As a child I had a passion for reading and always had a book in my hand. I was a big fan of Enid Blyton and her Adventures of the Famous Five, but my favourite was A.A. Milne's Christopher Robin and Winnie the Pooh. His stories were my first introduction to rhyme. I love daffodils so Milne's 'Daffodown Dilly' was another childhood favourite. From there I moved on to the epic 'Hiawatha' by Henry Wadsworth Longfellow. Fascinated by WW1 and the many poets that emerged out of it, I find 'Flanders Field' by John McCrea and 'Soldier' by Rupert Brook very poignant. I had always wanted to be a writer but life intervened. A busy mum of four children, I somehow never found the time. Now is my time

SALLY CHURCH
My husband has Parkinson's and it crept up on us slowly, subtly. Even the diagnoses took time. During that unknown

wait we began to look for signs. It was one evening, sitting in the garden he loves so much, that we realised he had lost his sense of smell. This inspired me to write the poem. I love poetry, my favourites being Tennyson and Keats and I particularly like Thomas Hardy. I dismissed Pam Ayres work but after seeing her performance hearing her recite her poems I was inspired by her, and wrote my poem.

It may seem light hearted and simple but it reflects some thoughts at the start of our PD journey.

ANDY CLEGG

A Yorkshire man born in Sheffield in August 1962, I am a divorcee with three children. I was diagnosed with Parkinson's Disease in October 2011 and started writing my poetry the following year. My poems reflect my daily life; in particular the battles and the struggles that living with Parkinson's presents.

AL FERBER

Septuagenarian from the backward colonies. Has written truck loads of poems starting 1968 n published in truck loads of poems in literary magazines starting 1972, 3 chaps books, 2 novels n 24 collections of poems. Put paint on canvas in non-representational manner last 16 years.

Given readings all over the map, at bars, art galleries, restaurants, colleges et al, all over the years.

Experienced wide variety of Parkinson symptoms persistently over 8 years. Hand tremors, loss of balance, sudden falls, hunched posture, head n body listing to the right, mouth gaping, drool dripping n more. Misdiagnosed: mild stroke, Parkinsonism, Parkinson's, Progressive Subnuclear Disorder (quick unthinkable death sentence) n more. 'Oops' said the medical profession – all side effects of medication. Simple sub tractions n eliminations ....

JOY LLOYD

Although I do not read poems every week and do not like all I read; poetry is the way I express myself. It is what reaches the deep places in me.

I have found that poetry allows the use of words to say something about the hardest or most wonder filled, the funniest and most incongruous events in life. When my husband was diagnosed with Parkinson's, it was a comfort to be able to write a few words that swelled and grew to fill the space and say the feelings. Poems, like emotions, have no regulation other than those you self impose.

The words melted in my mouth – that day, when a judge with a medical degree pronounced your life sentence – and mine; when I saw your face bleed tears, disbelief came to rescue – then grief, when your shaking hand had a name, belonged to another man-medic. Then words poured out of my eyes and my hands quivered and shook, like yours, and life started over again.

We have been married for longer than 33 years; everything we have experienced, we have done so together. Parkinson's is hard, but simple.

My name is Joy

HAZEL MORGAN

I do not regard myself as a poet. I have always liked writing poems from a young age but never thought they were any good, so I threw them all away. However some that I have written recently have been shown to friends who have encouraged me by saying they were good. I found my poem 'Mr PD' easy to write because it is about things that I am experiencing. I wrote this poem quickly, taking only about 15 minutes because it came from the heart.

COLIN PIDGLEY

Hi there, I'm Colin and I have Parkinson's Disease. I've always liked the challenge of playing around with words and reading poems from a variety of poets, including Pam Ayres, Spike Milligan and Adrian Plass who have influenced my writing. I hope my poems inspire others and show that, regardless of having Parkinson's, you can have a sense of humour and create something that makes others smile. That's my greatest ambition as a poet, to see beyond the disease and use the talents I have and to encourage others through the words I write, that anything is possible.

JAN SARGEANT

My interest in poetry developed in spite of a degree in English Literature and having read lots of dead, white male poets – with the occasional woman as an afterthought (it was the 70s). As a secondary teacher for many years and then as a teacher trainer, I wrote poetry in my spare time, some of it published.

Diagnosed with Parkinson's in May 2016, I avoid daytime TV by painting and writing poetry. I live in a conservation village with my husband and four cats, surrounded by art, poetry and plants. Parkinson's will never determine who I am; it's something to manage not be managed by. Writing poetry gives me a voice to explore all sorts of things and it's something everyone can have a go at. Just like painting. It's also very therapeutic and empowering. It's taken me a long time to throw off the confines of literary theory and just revel in language and all its wonderful richness. But I think I'm getting there.

BARRY WIGGINS

I began writing poetry whilst taking my school leaving exams in 1976. Growing up in the original punk era, I took to writing angry poems following John Cooper Clarke (the first punk poet). I seldom wrote again for more than 25 years, except the odd birthday or such. I really started to write more from the mid 2000's. One poem I wrote and read was at a Trade Union Conference to an audience of 1000 people. That's when I started to receive calls to write more. When I was diagnosed with Parkinson's I decided to encourage others to 'let go' in a Facebook forum where I and they can grow. I don't really have a form or style, because I never learnt them. I just experiment with styles I read or cobble them together.

DEBBIE WILLIAMS
My husband is the one with Parkinson's, but we both live with it every day.

I've written poetry since childhood, it has been my way of exploring and expressing deep emotional pain and traumatic life events.

JENNIFER YATES
I am a poet who happens to have Parkinson's Disease. I'm a Yorkshire woman several decades older than I'd like to be, living of all places in South East England. I write in different styles according to my mood and my reader. I love rhyme though my rhyming verse is usually written for fun, merely to amuse both myself and the reader. If I feel strongly enough about a subject then my words are more sober. I like a challenge and have played with different forms such as the pantoum. I love the War Poets, especially Henry Reed's 'Lessons of the War: The Naming of Parts' which I admit, I emulated recently with my poem about the corona virus pandemic. I also enjoy the poetry of Ian Macmillan, Benjamin Zephaniah and U.A. Fanthorpe to name but a few. I have studied a couple of creative

writing courses which had elements of poetic writing. I have recently had a poem published in conjunction with Jackie Morris for her latest work 'The Unwinding' which Morris describes as 'a companion, a talisman ..... and a place of respite from an increasingly frantic and complex world'. (Morris, J. 2020. 'The Unwinding.' Published by Unbound, London.)